# Ace

# I hit a hole-in-one!

# BOGEY

I'm having a bad day.

**DRIVE**

**Trust your swing, Brady.**

# Eagle

Eddie scored an Eagle!

# FORE

## Shout it as loud as you can, Margaux!

# Gimmie

**Sorry Nolan, that's not a gimmie.**

# Hook Shot

**Watch your elbow Jeff and check your grip.**

**I**ron

# Judging

Aidan judged the line perfectly and made the putt!

# Knee Knocker

## Larry missed. Oh no!

# Links

## Let's hit the links, Lucy!

# Mulligan

## Would you like a Mulligan?

# Nobbler

## Oh no, I nobbled.

# Out of Bounds

O-oh! Olivia, you went outside the boundaries.

# Penalty

Oh no! That's my third penalty this game!

# **R**ough

## I'm having a rough day.

# Shank

## You don't want that, Maeve.

# Vardon Grip

# **W**eather

Oh dear, it's raining... but the game must go on.

# X-outs

Oh no! These golf balls do not meet the manufacturer's standards.

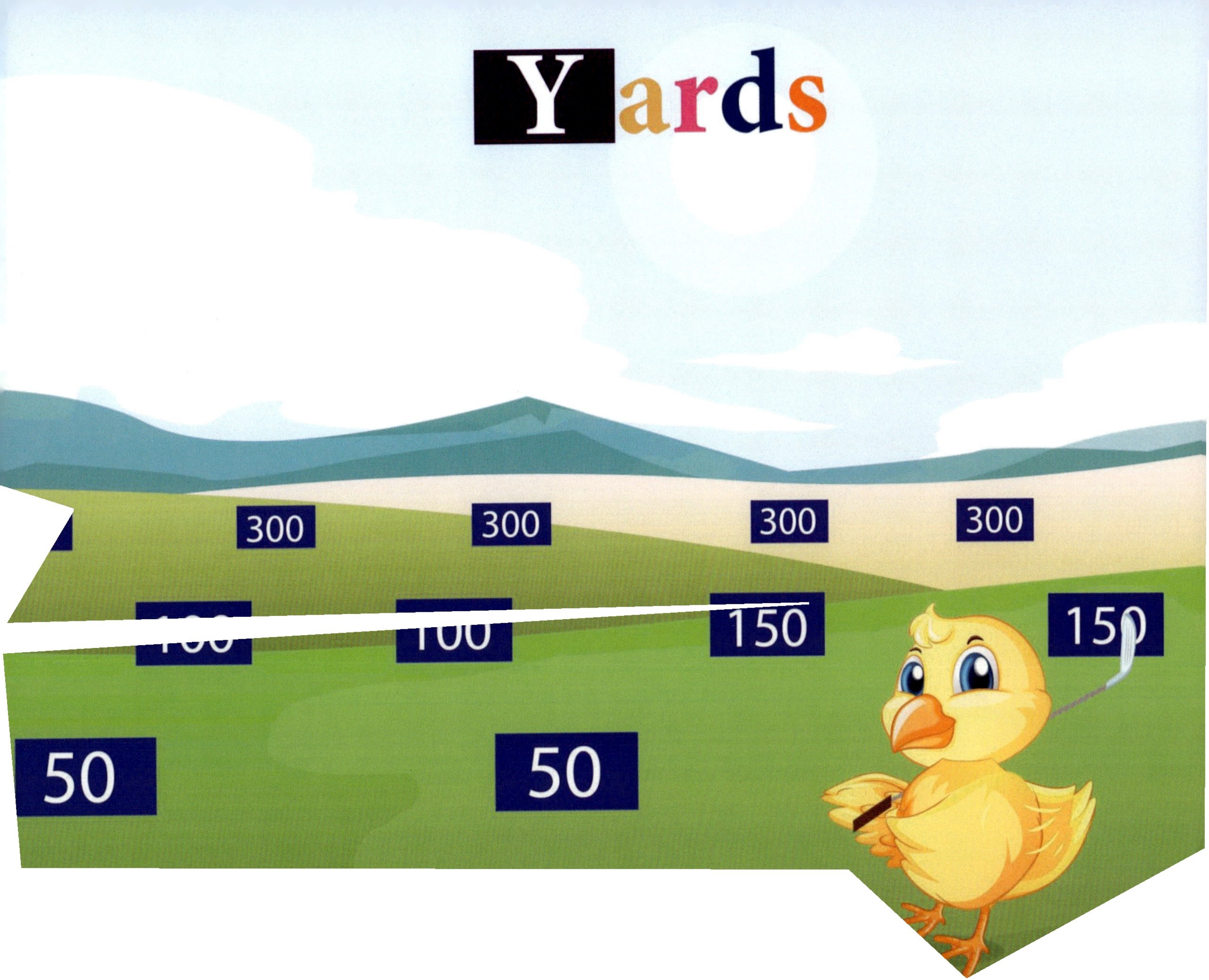

300    300    300    300

100    100    150    150

50           50

# Zoysia

This grass is itchy.